IS GOD
FOR REAL?

YOUTH FORUM SERIES

A YOUTH FORUM BOOK

IS GOD FOR REAL?

**by
Peter A. Bertocci**

THOMAS NELSON INC.
New York / Camden

ISBN: 0-8407-5317-9

Library of Congress Catalog Card Number: 75-169033

Printed in the United States of America

Foreword

This book is one of a series in a unique publishing effort in which Youth Research Center, Inc., Minneapolis, Minnesota, has joined with Thomas Nelson Inc., Camden, New Jersey. The books are based on the very real concerns, problems, aspirations, searchings and goals of young people today as measured by nation-wide surveys being conducted continuously by the research center.

Central to the series is the belief that we all have a compelling need to turn to a core of faith for guidelines in coping with the world in which we live. Each book deals with a specific need or concern of young people viewed in relation to the Christian faith. By drawing upon the results of the surveys, each author is helped to speak more directly to the conflicts, values and beliefs of today's young people.

The significance of this series is enhanced, as well, by the scholarship and commitment of the authors. The grasp of the field in which each writes lends authority to his work and has established this series as a basic reference eagerly read and appreciated by young people.

Contents

"I had heard thee by the hearing of my ears, but now my eyes see thee."

Job:42

"In religion we try to find an answer to the elementary question with which each one of us is newly confronted every morning, namely, what meaning and what value is to be ascribed to our life."

Albert Schweitzer

"Religion is a dangerous drug, unless it is wisely administered."

Borden Parker Bowne

IS GOD
FOR REAL?

Preface

I am addressing this book to those who like myself know the meaning of Harry Emerson Fosdick's words: "But some of the most wretched hours of my boyhood were caused by the pettiness and obscurantism, the miserable legalism and terrifying effects of fear that were associated with the religion of the churches."

This man who, whether we agree with him or not, helped many to see that the Bible was about what gives meaning to everyday living, said that when he was young. "My real struggle," he also said, "concerned the intellectual credibility of the Christian faith. Morally I went on trying to grow up, experimenting as youth must do, and learning by making a fool of myself as human beings always will. Intellectually, however, I faced a disturbing fight, from which I might have emerged minus religion." Later he asserted: "All the best meanings of personal religion could be mine without the crucifixion of the intellect."

He wrote his mother from college: "I'll behave as though there were a God, but mentally I am going to clear God out of the universe and start all over again to see what I can find. Even by this time, however, I was beginning to doubt some of my doubts."

* Harry Emerson Fosdick, *The Living of These Days*. Harper and Row, New York, 1956, pages 32, 53, 66.

Dr. Fosdick lived his active years in the first and middle years of the twentieth century. I have lived most of my life in the middle of the century, and year after year have faced young people, in and out of college, who literally made me feel like two cents. How could I, who was midway in life when a bomb exploded over Hiroshima, launching a new era—how could I who was trying to share my life with three growing sons, help them to live in the new world already in ferment? Underneath it all was the realization that society might not make it—or more candidly, perhaps I could not.

I would like to put the concern that runs through these pages in a more positive way. Many people today want to have a part in the new order that is in the making. Younger or older, they are wondering if the past has been outgrown; yet, there are many indications of their concern for a better world, a better way of doing things. In this book I wish to stress one basic belief upon which sincere, intelligent people throughout the world are divided: the belief that faith in any kind of God, and in any institution governed by that faith, must go. In the minds not of scoundrels but of well-informed, well-meaning people—people who want to put people first, not country or race—these questions press: Why not work to break down the walls between people? Why not stop these unending, divisive arguments over religion? Why not concentrate on being good persons, on creating a good society, on recreating a good, clean earth without too many people in it? Why not soft-pedal all other false "gods"?

An outstanding characteristic of our time is that both science and religion are being challenged in the name of the individual. In the middle half of the twentieth century, many idealists had turned to science as a surer way to the salvation of man than what they felt were nebulous and debatable religious beliefs. But by the late 1960's many had begun to see that science could make human life thing-like, expendable, ugly—and short.

Thus today, all over the world, every institution is being examined and challenged as men seek both the goods they believe are within their grasp through science. Maybe a better scientific perspective can lead them to the abundant life that their religious visions also spread before them. Yet men are not sure they can make it, either in the name of God or in the name of science.

I write this book in the conviction that this new ferment forces us to ask once more the basic questions about what it is that men must experience if they are to be creative and free. The great world religions differ, yet they all demand loyalty and obedience to a Supreme Being, or to Supreme Values, in order to find freedom and fulfillment. Too much is at stake, there is too much that we need to re-think as we seek new directions, for us not to understand what some of the basic issues are. But no one can stand in the shoes of his father or of posterity. We must think about life from where we are.

I shall, therefore, write of the experiences thinking men have had that were turning points in their concept of what made their lives worth living. Having said this, it may seem contradictory for me to turn to events in the Bible, but I think that there, and in the other great sacred books of the world we find the record of what I call turning-point experiences in the search for God.

If we take that record as the last word, and do not see that men much like ourselves are trying to tell us why they seek and what they find, it will be a dead word. When we find that there are conflicting records, we give up in despair or we keep on trying to patch things up, without entering into the search, the problem, the faith that inspired other searchers.

So in this small book I shall select from the past and the present, but always with a view to helping us see what the options are for us in our own lives.

1. Can We Find God in the Midst of Conflict?

Please do not read another sentence if you want a fool-proof answer to the question: What gives meaning to my life, or to anyone else's life? If you do read on, I invite you to face with me some experiences that others like you and me have faced all through the history of man. We may not agree with each other in the end, but I would not write this if I did not think that the attempt to understand our own turning-point experiences is more important than agreement.

A turning-point, or basic, experience is my term for an important change of direction in a person's life. It is a turning-point not simply because we undergo it but because it raises a question which can only be resolved as we change or redirect our lives. It need not come suddenly. Yet, something happens and our own past and our future take on a new look.

In this chapter I wish to describe several experiences that could be momentous turning-points in a person's life.

One young American had such an experience on a street in Cairo, Egypt. He and his father, a college professor, went to a travel agency in Cairo to arrange for the trip to the pyramids. On the way they were approached by boys who insisted on shining their shoes or just begging. While the father was having his shoes shined, an old man tried to sell him a relatively worthless item. The father finally gave him a dollar. The boys took this as a cue that more dollars would be forthcoming and they pursued the father and son down the street.

Suddenly the father heard his son sob and saw that tears were streaming down his cheeks. Hoping to reassure him, the father explained that one had to expect these things in areas of great poverty. His son turned to him and exclaimed, "Oh, it's not that. I want to know why I should be born in America and in your family, why I should not be one of these boys and any of them not be me." How blind the father had been! For his son this was a turning-point experience. He saw himself in a new light, and he now lives with a new sense of responsibility about what he considers "mine" and "theirs."

But this *is* a basic question: Why should I have been born where I was, with my advantages and disadvantages, a male or a female, black or yellow or white, with certain abilities and disabilities? Whatever the answer to this question, each of us is still faced by the fact that he is what he is and that he is different from others. But there is another fact which is ignored. None of us can say that he deserves either all the good that is his, or all the bad. Even if there is no answer to the question of why anyone of us is here, perhaps, since we choose to stay, the question we face is this: What will make our stay worthwhile?

*   *   *

In facing this issue, I wish to examine a turning-point in the life of a great leader of men.

A son was born to a Hebrew woman at a time when the Egyptian government had decreed that all the sons of her people would be killed at birth so that no member of this enslaved people would ever become powerful enough to pose a threat to the pharaoh of Egypt. The Hebrew mother, hoping to evade the edict, took her newborn son, Moses, and hid him in the reeds on the banks of the Nile. There he was found by Pharaoh's daughter when she came to bathe. Moses became her ward, and his mother became his nurse.

It does not matter here whether the details of the story of Moses and his relationship to his family and to his people, to Pharaoh, to the Egyptians, and to God, were exactly as the Bible cites them. What is more important is the drama which unfolds and which, I hope to show, speaks to each of us who is facing the question: What makes my life worth living?

Moses grew up in a palace, with the education and the privileges accorded a ward of a princess. But Moses, as a young man, eventually came to the turning-point—the crossroads in his life—as do each of us, no matter where or how we grow up.

One day Moses saw two men fighting. One was an Egyptian, and the other a Jew. Reared in the Egyptian atmosphere of Pharaoh's palace but by his Jewish mother, his nurse, who must have taught him much about his Jewish heritage, Moses had to face the question: "Who am I, a Jew or an Egyptian?" Did he also ask "What do I do about what I think is unfair, and why?" Decisions about right and wrong are not neat choices; so often mixed loyalties are involved.

I cite the Revised Standard Version of the biblical account in Exodus 2:11 f:

"One day, when Moses had grown up, he went out to his people and looked on their burdens; and he saw an Egyptian beating a Hebrew, one of his people. He looked this way and that, and seeing no one he killed the Egyptian and hid him in the sand. When he went out the next day, behold, two Hebrews were struggling together; and he said to the man that did the wrong, 'Why do you strike your fellow?' He answered, 'Who made you a prince and a judge over us? Do you mean to kill me as you did the Egyptian?' Then Moses was afraid, and thought, 'Surely the thing is known.' When Pharaoh heard of it, he sought to kill Moses. But Moses fled from Pharaoh, and stayed in the land of Midian. . . ."

Did Moses flee only because he was afraid of being caught, or was there another reason? I think so. For his first decision to favor a Hebrew against an Egyptian would not help him when he saw one Jew fighting another. The Jew flung at him the question no thinking person can escape: "Who made you a judge over us?" It always comes as a shock when we are challenged by those we have tried to help.

Moses behaved as many of us would behave. Challenged, confused, frightened, he ran. It seemed so clear to him that he could not stand by while one person hurt another unjustly. It also was impossible, evidently, for him to explain why he interfered. What is interesting is that Moses could not run from this question. According to the biblical record, Moses interfered again on behalf of the Midian maidens when shepherds drove them away from the well to which the women had come for water. He not only intervened, but helped the maidens water their father's flock. Soon Moses married one of the maidens and became a prosperous shepherd. If being well-married and financially secure were the essence of the good life, Moses had a good life. But plainly, he could not run away from himself and those questions: Can I stand still when I see injustice? On what grounds do I intervene when I can always be asked: "Who made you a judge over me?"

Here is one of the fundamental reasons so many sensitive men have come to know God, and why others have been led to deny him. But let us take a second look at the issue that was a turning-point in Moses' life, and ask ourselves how it applies to us and our lives.

First, can we intervene in a dispute on the side of what we regard as justice, because we like or dislike one antagonist more than the other? Clearly, our opponent could ask: "Just because you don't like me, am I wrong?" Second, can we settle the matter of justice or injustice by fighting it out? Is the winner right because he won? Does might, in other words, make right?

Is there a difference if I move from my own likes or dislikes to those of my family, my ethnic group, or my country? If the people of one nation say their country has the right to intervene in the lives of the citizens of another country, is the psychology or the logic any different?

Here, then, we come to a key issue, for it is clear to me that anyone who chooses on the basis of power alone is morally blind.

There is another issue we should raise. If might alone never makes right in human affairs, would the answer be different if one said, "It's right because God says so"? If one says that an act is right because God's power alone is behind it, then I must reply, "That's the Devil, not God."

I am not asserting that Moses went through this reasoning process, but it is clear from the following incident that he was on the side of the underdog. I cite another great moment in history, as recorded in Exodus 2:23 f.

"And the people of Israel groaned under their bondage, and cried out for help, and their cry under bondage came up to God. And God heard their groaning . . . and God knew their condition.

"Now Moses was keeping the flock of his father-in-law, Jethro, the priest of Midian; and he led his flock to the west side of the wilderness, and came to Horeb, the mountain of God. And the angel of the Lord appeared to him in a flame of fire out of the midst of a bush; and he looked, and lo, the bush was burning, yet it was not consumed. And Moses said, 'I will turn aside and see this great sight, why the bush is not burnt.'

"When the Lord saw that he turned aside to see, God called to him out of the bush, 'Moses, Moses!' And he said, 'Here am I.' . . . Then the Lord said, 'I have seen the affliction of my people who are in Egypt, and have heard their cry because of their task masters; I know their sufferings. . . . Come, I will send you to Pharaoh, that you may bring forth my people, the sons of Israel, out of Egypt . . .'."

In this experience Moses found the assurance that he was not alone in his condemnation of slavery and his concern for the plight of the Israelites. In this call to him to free his people, he was to deal with both Jew and Egyptian and to act in God's name, not his own, and not even in the name of the Jews.

We must not let this point go unnoticed: the struggle was in Moses' life; the bush that burned and wasted not was invisible to others; it was Moses alone who heard God. We often hear that God deals with people, but he deals with them in their own lives; he encounters them at certain growing-points in their lives, and what each experiences is not a once-for-all-time experience, or answer to a problem. In the very presence of God's call, Moses was still worried by his gnawing question. He said to God, "Who am I that I should go to Pharaoh, and bring the Sons of Israel out of Egypt?" And God said: "But I will be with you . . ."

One feels for Moses as he realized what was being asked of him. Anyone who asks, "Who am I?", often is brought up short by the realization that he is one of whom much is demanded. He asks, also, whether or not he can do all this, is he alone in this? For Moses the reassurance came: "I will be with you."

But even this did not quiet Moses. The inner struggle was too much for him, and he asked:

"If I come to the people of Israel and say to them,'The God of your fathers has sent me to you,' and they ask me, 'What is his name?' What shall I say to them? God said to Moses, 'I am who I am'" (The original is also translated as, "*I am what I am*," or, "*I will be what I will be.*")

Again, I see in this passage the Moses who was still aware that people will ask him, "Who made you a prince and a judge over us?" And I am suggesting that in this turning-point experience with God, Moses saw that he can go to his suffering people and say, "Not I, Moses, but God demands justice." For Moses, God was not "up there" hurling his thunderbolts in anger and majesty, imposing his will upon men without regard for their needs but to prove, instead, his sovereignty. He was the heartbeat of the universe, making himself felt in Moses' own heartbeat for the oppressed.

Yet the struggle for justice was not to be easy because it was to be a struggle for men's hearts. Indeed, Moses was soon to feel despair about his cause and his leadership. Later, when his people had escaped from Pharaoh, when they faced the heat of the desert and other hardships, they complained and they asked: "Why did you lead us out of Israel? Better had we died in Egypt."

Although they listened to Moses and heard him out of their hopes and their despair, they did not clearly grasp what he was trying to tell them about God's ways. When

Moses retreated to Mount Sinai and returned with the Ten Commandments, he found that they were worshipping a golden calf. Had he not been convinced that, no matter how fickle was their faith, these were still the children of God for whom God cared, would he not have run again?

I have been trying to use Moses' experience to illustrate one way in which the awareness of God becomes a vital faith—a commitment that helps a man endure uncertainties. For he is committed to a vast plan that keeps life full, rather than aimless, empty and shallow.

I have chosen experiences involving great injustices of life as turning-points because I wish to raise another question: Can it be that my conviction that injustice is wrong is only mine? What would happen to me if I gave my life to upholding justice and those I wished to help were ungrateful and unappreciative of my efforts? In the course of such excruciating debates, in the midst of self-doubt and uncertainty about the meaning of life, there can come to a man who is honest with himself about the good and evil in life the conviction that he is not alone in his concern for justice, that no one should be the victim of injustice. Why? Because injustice does not permit a person to grow and fulfill himself in this world.

You and I will come to know who and what we are only as we take moral issues so seriously that we ask: "Can it be that we are alone in caring?" For millions the answer has been "No," even though they might disagree on details. But this answer is not written across the skies. It is, as Kant said, "the moral law within" that reflects the moral structure of things, the "I am what I am" which we call God.

2. Is Experiencing God the Great Illusion?

There are many ways in which people come to an awareness that there "must be" a God. This need not be the result of a long list of arguments placed like numbers upon a sheet of paper and then added up to give a sum. This was hardly the way in which Moses came alive to God. God was there, calling to him out of the burning bush.

The Bible, of course, takes it for granted that God exists, but we are asking a different question: "How do we come to be so certain that there is a God?" When we get beneath the surface and try to understand who we are and what we stand for, we see that we stand for the nature of things upon which we depend. This includes our own basic nature, which we did not create. The burning-bush —which you and I might not have seen—symbolized something in Moses' life.

You may ask: "But don't you believe that the voice actually spoke, that the flame, which did not burn the bush, was there? Or do you think Moses imagined it all?"

I can only say that I think this experience was to Moses as real an experience as he ever had, but that the burning bush is not to be thought of as we think of a light that is there for all to see—the effect of electricity in the sky. Nor was it like a dream that we can explain by our own past experiences and which takes over while our minds and bodies are asleep.

For each of us, our own "burning bush" may not be a burning bush at all. When we struggle deeply enough with a moral problem, a drama may enact itself which is not make-believe but is instead the playing out of the realization that this is the way things are. The story of the burning bush, then, is not a fairy tale; it is a record of one man's realization that he was not living in a world that was devoid of caring.

I have tried to show how the search for meaning in life goes on. I have tried to show that we all face a basic question: Either we live with others by like and dislike, by power and fear, or we live with others "under God"—and that is the way we are made to live, even if we do not do so. The choice is ours, but I suggest that the latter choice is too important not to be ours, not to be worth all we can give it.

* * *

Now let us consider a view of man's belief in God that is completely different from my interpretation of Moses' experience. I might call it the Good News According to Freud. Briefly, I shall set out a family of ideas with one central conviction behind them: Men experience God but the God they experience does not exist, even though they go on "experiencing" him.

Every thinking person, whether he believes in God or not, will wonder whether the experience of God tells us more about man's deep wishes than it does about things as they really are. In his book, *The Future of an Illusion*, Sigmund Freud called religion just that—an illusion. But many readers miss the despair Freud was trying to suggest by his title. An illusion is an experience we have when we keep on seeing something in the same way, even though reason tells us it is not that way. For example, we see parallel tracks converging in the distance even though we know they do not.

Freud was saying that the experience of a certain kind of God will persist, alas, because people will keep on seeing themselves in a certain way, and thus in seeing God in a certain way, too. But he doesn't exist in fact, Freud said, despite their need to believe. Similarly, those who believe that "religion is the opiate of the people" do not deny that many people seem to need opiates. They simply urge that people learn to live without an "escape."

The experience of religion is not to be taken lightly, for it arises from deep conflicts in man. Nevertheless, in the Freudian view this is the wrong way of dealing with conflicts; religion will keep a man in his infancy when he should be putting away dreams that keep him from facing reality.

Yet there is something in the human predicament that no one can escape. We cannot think about God without thinking about man. We cannot "see" God without paying attention to ourselves as perceivers. This idea is put to work in a tempting way by those who claim that man knows God only as he knows an illusion. This description of the human situation goes like this: A human being is so helpless at birth that, left to himself, he would die. He depends upon mother and father, in particular, and on the physical world and society to keep him alive. As he grows he learns not only what he must do to insure the goodwill of his parents and of society but also how to comply with the laws of nature. He comes to realize that the customs of others—his family, his friends, his larger social group—as well as the laws of his city, state, and nation spell out the basic rules for living with others.

These say to him: Whether we feel like it or not, whether you feel like it or not, we demand at least this kind of behavior, and we pay to have the police and the courts see to it that we all are judged equally before the law. Thus every person is born into a system of rules and customs that are themselves the result of people trying to live with each other in a physical environment which does not give them too many alternatives.

What, you ask, has this to do with the idea of God?

As the Freudian sees it, this interaction between child, parents, society, and nature sets up strong tensions and anxieties. In the first place, the child soon learns that if he is to get what *he* wants, he must not only conform to his parents' and society's wishes, but often postpone what he wants, or actually sacrifice it. In Freud's view of human nature, the need to have as much power as possible is so strong that the child has a hard time controlling it, even when he wants to, and adults know this.

What can be done? Pressure from adults must be strengthened so that each person knows it just won't pay, in terms of pleasure and pain, to let himself go. Thus parents and society must work together so that each new member of society finds that the fear of the rod, of custom, of law, has become second nature to him—an inner "conscience" that keeps him conforming and sacrificing.

At the same time, in the Freudian view, the individual is asked to give up so much that the barriers against the drive for pleasure must be as strong as possible. We already use society and the state to back up the parents. Why not take the next step and back up society with the will of God? We are back at a slightly different version of Moses' question: In whose name, indeed, does society ask the individual to make the sacrifices he finds so difficult?

In the name of a God of justice who will not long brook disorder and disloyalty; if in this life he defies that will, he cannot escape the wrath of God in the next life.

The system seems perfect—if only we can teach it correctly and enforce it, say the Freudians. Make God look benign, call him "Father" and make it clear that all will go well if one makes the necessary sacrifices. Put this simply, it looks like a hoax, a scheme for oppressing the individual at the expense of others.

But life isn't that simple, and even at our best we human beings are so weak. No matter how clever we are, we still get sick, we still are at the mercy of the physical world, and none of us can escape death, although we may try to minimize the fact of death, or harden ourselves to it, or resolve to go out mad. As Dylan Thomas wrote: "Do not go gentle into that good night—Rage, rage against the dying of the light." * The forces of nature—earthquakes, cancer, mental illness—will not bend to our pleading and so we say (still according to the Freudians), "Why not play it safe and perhaps achieve some peace of mind?"

Doesn't all this seem contrived? Think about a small boy who sees his mother as his source of security. He knows she may exact some sacrifices from him, but he also knows she needs him, too, and that he has the power to hurt her. And so the youngster adjusts to his mother. But whatever peace of mind he finds is disturbed by the realization that his mother also needs and loves his all-powerful father. The boy then may come to hate that father, and he becomes more anxious than ever. His security is gone, but he fears expressing the rebellion he feels.

* *Collected Poems of Dylan Thomas,* New York, New Directions Book, 1957, p. 128.

And so he declares that he loves his father, he tries hard to get along well with him, for he knows this will please his mother, too, and he will be secure. After awhile, this all becomes second nature, and the boy lives by this "settlement" as part of an unconscious code.

So with our relationship with God—indeed, all the more so. For hasn't God also been used by mother and father, by society, even by the boy's conscience, as a way of making him accept the system and conform, even though the boy inwardly churns with rebellion? In the case of God, it is even worse, for although he cannot be seen, he is everywhere. Thus, "the fear of the Lord is the beginning of wisdom" comes to mean: God is the cosmic bogey-man, the cosmic policeman—but the cosmic insurance policy, too. If I cannot escape from his all-seeing eye, the boy begins to think, neither can those who might harm me. The solution, then, is to live in conformity with God's will.

I cannot emphasize enough that this picture of God—one that is so natural, so easy to acquire, especially when one is growing up—probably has been shared by millions of people for thousands of years. It appeals to that part of us that needs to feel there is an ultimate justice for all, that there is a pilot at the helm who knows everything there is to know, and that we can rely upon him.

This is why Freud said that religion is not something we can just put aside, that we need to keep reminding ourselves that religion is untrue to fact, that we must not depend on this illusion.

Critics of religion, dating back to Epicurus, the Greek philosopher, put Freud's point of view in other ways. We keep on thinking, they say, that we can live with our own fears of death, and even with the problems, the blatant injustices of this world, by focusing on another life beyond death that will guarantee freedom from all this. And, they continue, we therefore spend our time and energy trying to figure out how we can stay on the right side of God, how we can save our souls, how we can, as it were, bribe God into letting us off lightly in the next world. The result is that we don't concentrate on *improving this world,* on seeing to it that we create a "heaven on earth."

This is the meaning of the phrase, "religion is the opiate of the people." It not only dulls people into accepting their lot, but puts the all-knowing yet inscrutable will of God behind selfishness, indifference, and apathy to social change. Because of the inscrutability of God's will, it is easy for anyone to decide that God's will is on his side of any social issue. The result is that "in the name of God" every social evil has found supporters, whether it be the proper relation of whites to non-whites, of men to women, of workers to their employers, of citizens to the state. It has even divided world religions, Hindus from Buddhists, Moslems from Christians, and set many Christians against one another—each group professing a special revelation of the will of God. The result is the divided world we have to live in, but the divisions are made worse by the fact that they are supported by sincere people who think that anyone who disagrees with them will one day see the light.

This is a brief outline of what might be called the great Humanist rebellion. We must take it seriously if we are to understand the "great illusion" and free our minds of its spell. We must reject the imposition upon us of a will that is not our own, say the Humanists. We must realize that an experience like that of Moses', in which God was revealed as someone who cared about the freedom of the Jews, was no more than Moses' longing for some source of

authority beyond himself in order to justify his interference in the affairs of other men.

It is well to understand this plan for a kingdom of men
on earth, because it is attracting many sincere, concerned,
and scholarly thinkers. It seems clear that Freud and the
Humanists are saying that, once we tear the blinders of
religious faith from our eyes, we shall see that it is up to
man to help himself. He cannot do this unless he faces
reality, and not God. He must see that children are brought
up by parents who understand how insecure a child can be,
that it is human nature for a child who feels insecure to
grasp at any way of life that will give him as much security
as possible. Parents will be more likely to mis-educate
their children if they themselves feel desperate in the face
of the hardships of life, and they will continue to do so
until they band with others in society to protect the weak
and the worthy against those who by ability and power—
ruthless or not—protect themselves first.

How will this take place? It will not be easy. Basically,
it will involve trust in man, and a willingness to give up
immediate gratifications for the sake of satisfying long-
run needs. This, however, cannot be done unless we put
reason first, as a guide to our emotional natures.

As I have said, any intelligent person in the contempo-
rary world must take seriously this Humanist view of salvation without God. Yet one thing must be said, if we
are to be honest with history. Many believers in God
have been the strongest critics of superstition and obscurantism, and they certainly have been the exponents of
social change. They have insisted that an inner and con-
stant problem of religion is the ability to be self-critical, to
make sure that belief in God is not an escape from the
hard, practical issues. To attack religion as the opiate of

the people is as unfair as attacking science for the use to which society has put the discoveries that pollute the air and the water.

It is possible to say that the way out is to improve the human condition through science only if we select those facts which favor this point of view. If we are to be fair, there is opportunity both through science and religion for improving the human condition. Gadgets and instruments for both preserving and for destroying life are no more the necessary consequences of the search for truth than are "escapism" and "self-righteousness" the necessary consequences of search for faith. There have been deeply dedicated humanitarians among both atheists and theists. Our question, therefore, must be this: "Is there reason for believing in God? And does the God we can believe in support dedication to justice and mercy and truth?"

3. Not God, but Which God?

The word "God" means different things to different people. In this chapter, we will make a start on describing the kind of a God in whom I think we can believe. We will explore the evidence later. However, it seems to me that no thinking person can say, without being confronted with some rather troublesome questions: "I believe in Something behind it all." Does this "Something" favor justice and mercy? Is this "Something" a being that knows what is going on, and does "It" care? How is this "Something" related to the electrons of the earth, to the galaxies in the universe? To believe in God, in other words, is to believe in a Being whose nature makes it possible for us to understand our experience as a whole.

Yet many people ask how can we ever define God adequately? Can we find a reasoned, capsule description into which we can pour the grandeur of God? The answer is that we cannot define anything so completely that nothing more remains to be said.

No matter what I say about God on the basis of evidence I now have, I must be willing to revise my view once there is new evidence. Thus I must reply that God is more than we will ever know, but to believe in God is to believe in a certain kind of God until we find reason to revise this idea.

It has been fashionable in some quarters to emphasize

the mystery of God, but I must refuse to allow the mystery to obscure the evidence. Nothing but mystery follows mystery, so if we take this view seriously, let us then stop talking about the difference that mystery has made in our lives.

I will begin, then, to outline the view of God which I think is not only consistent with what we know but also makes what we know fit together.

1. God is a Person. He is the Supreme Person on which every other being depends both for its existence and its continuance. It is so easy to misunderstand what it means to call God a Supreme Person that we should clarify this.

2. God, we may now add, is the Creator-Person, whereas all human persons are created-creators. That is, finite persons do not create themselves, and when they, in turn, "create," they are limited to what is at hand—stone, paint, iron ore, earth, and so on.

3. God is morally perfect. He creates, sustains, and co-operates with a view to producing what is most worthwhile. Nothing would seem to be beyond his power as Creator; he is omnipotent. How is his sovereign power related to his moral perfection? God, in his goodness, cannot and will not make every evil become a "good." He allows evil to occur, because he also has created man free with the opportunity to choose between good and evil.

For example, an all-good, all-powerful God would not, I take it, change the properties of water the moment a person is about to drown. Free persons depend upon the properties of water always remaining the same. To change them, or to change the causes of drowning would not give us a dependable world in which to live.

Similarly, would we reasonably expect a good God to change the laws of physics because valiant astronauts, who are depending on those laws, are in trouble because of some failure in their space craft's electrical system? This relationship between the power and the goodness of any being, God included, is not a simple one, and we must come back to it. But let us note the importance of it for prayer.

How often people pray to God, in all earnestness and for unselfish ends, without an answer to that for which they pray. But would the God of all the people be a good God if he answered the prayers of those who, in desperate straits, were asking him to change the laws on which everybody had been depending and would continue to depend?

The laws of nature and of human nature may well be God's promises to us that if A happens, then B may be expected to happen. God has established an order by which we all can live, and his goodness consists not in yielding to special pleading, but rather in helping to create a new relationship between himself and those he loves and who care for him.

I am far from denying the importance of prayer. But I am suggesting that we always must ask ourselves whether we want to be on God's side, rather than demand that he be on ours if that would hurt others.

People like to say that God is perfect and assume that, being omnipotent, he can do anything. But they are thinking like one of my children who once assumed his father could do anything. The boy had broken a phonograph record, and he tearfully pleaded with me to fix it. When I said I could not, he cried out: "Oh, Dad, please fix it. Put a nail in it."

So people have sometimes, in what they thought was

the proper awe of God, held that God is first and fore-
most omnipotent. Taken literally, this means the "power
to do everything." But they have not thought through
"everything." Do they mean that God could make a mountain without a valley? Make a square out of a circle?
Make 2 plus 2 equal 5? What good purpose would thus be
accomplished, even if it made sense to anybody? Omnipotence, then, means that God can do everything consistent with his goodness and has the power to do everything worthwhile. For example, if it is worthwhile to
create persons who also will be free to create within limits
—and I shall hold that this is *most* worthwhile—then
God will do so. We are seeing that we must understand
God's attributes in relationship to each other. There is another attribute: omniscience.

4. God knows all there is to know; he is omniscient.
There are two points to bear in mind here. First, God is
aware of all that is going on in this world, and all that can
go on. Second, God's awareness is *at least* non-
contradictory to ours. Sometimes people who dwell on the
omnipotence and mystery of God are likely to paint themselves into a corner. They say: "God's ways are not our
ways, and his Being stretches so far beyond anything we
can comprehend that nothing we say can have any basic
application to him." But they hesitate when we ask, "Can
2 plus 2 equal 4 for us and not for God?" "Can our white
be his black?" "Can injustice for us be justice for him?"
Surely not. God may not measure in miles or by the time
astronomers use, but if we can measure with any success—
and we can—surely our measure does not contradict God's.

There is one problem over which great minds have ago-
nized. They have wanted to say that an omnipotent, om-

niscient Creator could, of course, know all the future as he knows the past. Therefore, could he not then predict everything that could occur and control it if he willed?

Let us agree that where the physical world is concerned —the regularity of the movements of stars and planets, for instance, which even we understand—God does have predictive knowledge. But where people and their God-given freedom of choice are concerned, can God know what choice will be made?

For example, John has chosen to mix sand, stones, and cement, but has not yet poured water into the mixture. God, I assume, will know exactly what can happen to the mixture, how soon it will harden, how strong it will be. I also assume that God knows so much about John that he can predict whether or not John will pour in the water. But suppose that John is having a hard time deciding whether he ought to prepare that mix. Will God be able to predict every detail of what John will do? My own answer is "No," but many great thinkers have believed that this answer would deny God's omnipotence and leave the destiny of each person and the history of the world beyond God's control.

Still it seems clear to me that if God delegated to man limited freedom, and if freedom meant that man must be the author of his own fate within circumscribed limits, then this means that God does not know exactly what a man will do until he does it.

This is not to say that God does not know all the alternatives open to man, or that God cannot or will not influence man in ways consistent with man's freedom. But to the extent that man is free to make up his own mind and to act upon his own decisions, to that extent God does not know *exactly* what man will do. If God has limited himself in granting this freedom, for God to interfere would mean that man really is not free. A father cannot grant his son freedom to use the family car, but make it impossible to buy gas, and still say he believes in freedom for his son. At the same time, the son cannot complain when he forgets that driving too fast can mean trouble for him.

Not "God," then, but which God? I have been trying to show that we cannot easily describe God's nature. His omnipotence means that nothing that exists could be what it is without him, and he does not limit his own power by creating other persons who are free only within limits. Indeed, we call God good because we believe that, in the main, we do have a hand in what we make of ourselves in a world whose order can be trusted.

However, it seems, we cannot get along without images and symbols. Symbols are short cuts; they stand for something it would take a long time to explain. Cupid is love, Santa Claus is the spirit of Christmas, an eagle a symbol of America. If we forget that symbols—the term, "father," as applied to God, for instance—are just that and if we take them literally, we can be misled. So with the father symbol in mind, we may ask: "Does God have a white beard and a stern or a benevolent look?" When symbols are actions—such as saluting the flag, tipping one's hat, shaking hands—they can become lifeless rituals. If symbols are to fulfill their purpose, we must stop from time to time and ask what it is they are trying to suggest, to bring nearer to us.

People often think they honor God more by saying that he is a Being "beyond all our knowledge." What they probably mean is that nothing we can say will be adequate. This is readily admitted. But can we thus avoid the responsibility for the best symbol our knowledge allows? When we refer to God as a Being, the most we are saying is that he is continuous with the best kind of being we know.

We would do better to take a cue from the writer of the first chapter of Genesis. God, he says, after having created the order of the world and the animals, used a model when he made man. God made man in his own image. Why did this writer say this? Did he realize that, unlike any thing or animal, man meant to bring the Creator of the heavens and the earth closer to man? No, a being like man, he speculated, must be nearer to an infinite person than to animals or plants. Thus, he said, man was made "in the image of God," the Planner and Creator of the universe.

Our knowledge will never be adequate, but it does make sense to say that God is a unity, that he knows what he is about, and that his activities in the world express his nature. In this sense, God is a person.

The greater question now is this: Can we find reasonable grounds for holding that a Person-Creator who is good does exist?

4. Does Faith in Nature Point to God?

You, no doubt, like myself have lost your way in a strange city. We approach someone and ask directions. We assume he lives there and knows his way around. We would be startled if he answered us in another language that we do not understand. It comes as a surprise, then, when we realize that in approaching someone else, we have made certain assumptions about him. Because his body is like ours, we *assume* a common background. We also *assume* that he will understand our problem because we *assume* he knows what it means to be lost. We *assume* he will not be offended by our approaching him, that he is willing to help someone else. All along, clearly, we are using our own experience as a standard for guiding our action in relation to him and others; that is, we proceed by *reasonable analogy*, based upon what we know about ourselves.

Let us take a closer look at this process, for I shall argue in this chapter that man's mind is not alien to reality. *Man, in knowing his world, discovers that his intelligence can cope with the world.*

In our time, there have been two scientific developments which have challenged the basic harmony between our minds and reality. When scientists undertook to go to the moon, they made the assumption, grounded in other knowledge and assumptions that seemed well-established, that, despite differences, the laws governing the moon's environment were enough like those governing the earth as to warrant the expenditure of man's effort and resources. And so exploration began. After several unmanned flights, it seemed reasonable to risk the lives of well-trained, well-equipped, and daring astronauts. They could not proceed without preparation for the possibility of vast differences between earth and moon. They also needed the coordination of the efforts of thousands of their fellowmen, all governed by the same faith in the project. Faith in ourselves and these missions also was based on faith in nature and her unchangeable laws.

Let me use another dramatic example: heart-transplants. The medical profession is dedicated to the use of knowledge for the preservation of life. A skilled specialist decides that the time has come to try to transplant the heart of a person who has just died into the body of a patient whose own heart will not function much longer. The unknowns still are many, but what is known inspires confidence that the patient may live a longer life with the transplant. He and his family then decide whether or not the risks are worth taking. Note once more that we move to an unknown on the basis of what is known. Although, at this writing it seems that the resistance of the patients' bodies is greater than was realized, patients with transplanted hearts also have had difficulty surviving because of other factors, unique to each case.

But note the assumption throughout: if we observe nature carefully, and if we obey the cause-and-effect sequences she teaches us to expect, we will find her faithful. This means that we may trust our own minds to fathom her secrets, provided we don't try to dictate to her. Properly disciplined, our minds do not work at cross purposes with nature, although we may make mistakes.

Can we draw a further conclusion? If the human mind probes a nature it did not create and finds that its probing is honored with new knowledge, is it not possible that a cosmic Mind is at work supporting our disciplined search?

I suggested in the last chapter that God is a Creator-Person, whose mind is at work in his world. Nature is tremendously complex; yet its events fit into a pattern that makes more sense if it can be seen not as the result of aimless movements but as the work of a cosmic Planner. What we are saying when we explore a world that we believe to be orderly is that there is a mind-like quality about nature, and that is one aspect of God. To put it differently, the indomitable faith of the scientist that the world he studies is a world that reveals itself to him is evidence for belief in a cosmic Mind. In science we live in the faith that this world we know is one order of events to which our minds are not alien. Is this not a beginning of belief in one knowing Person at the heart of things? A beginning, yes.

5. Can We Believe in Freedom and Justice Without Believing in God?

Is it possible that the world supports and influences man's search for truth but not his search for a life that is worth living? How do we answer this question?

Obviously, no voice will cry out from the heavens to tell us once and for all that our logic and mathematics, that our scientific procedures fit in with reality. As we try to stay alive and to understand our world, we must reshape our methods of acquiring knowledge.

It may help us to think of how a child grows to know his mother. Each makes demands upon the other, but as they discover the truth about each other, they also influence each other up to a point. When we drink water to quench our thirst, we, up to a point, change the properties of that water as it affects our bodies.

Can we not say the same thing about goodness, or what we call our values? I think we can. Our goodness is ours; values or the lack of them cannot exist without us. It is we who are just or unjust, merciful or merciless. Is this not true, also, of good and evil? I believe it is. Human beings sift experiences involving values and disvalues, and in this sifting and sorting other people play an important part in helping us discover the values that are most worthwhile, that are especially important in this world. More than that, we cannot know what experiences are valuable to us, and we cannot ourselves become all that we could be without other people, and without our influencing them, also, as we develop.

Thus our values, our ways of experiencing ourselves in relation to others and to the world, are true and dependable in the same basic way as our knowledge of nature is true and dependable. That is, we weigh relationships with others and find that some are so important that our lives have no meaning without them.

We also realize that we have few, if any, value-experiences that are not connected to a system that includes the value-experiences of others. Our enjoyment of health, of play, of knowledge, of beauty, of friendship, are not only interwoven in our own lives but they influence and are influenced by other people, and by the physical world in which we live.

Are there some values which form a sturdy foundation for all other values? I am going to name four: creativity, mutual understanding, justice, and forgiveness. They at once presuppose the value of wisdom. Without them every other value in life is endangered; with them, every other value is enhanced.

By *creativity* I mean the willingness to discipline oneself by one's ideals. Others may not agree with my ideals; I may find that my ideals change. But they represent my conception of what values are good for me. I find myself feeling that, whatever else my duty is, it is to control my thoughts and actions by my ideals. Creativity, everywhere in human life, is not freedom from restraint, it is the will to restrain ourselves as best as we can. We know how we detest the feeling that we cannot control ourselves when the going gets rough. We may despise what another person stands for, but we cannot but respect his willingness to stand and be counted.

Come to think of it, creativity is the only value that depends entirely upon ourselves. Creativity is that self-determination to move with everything in our power to see that what we think is right is done. Creativity directly involves our freedom to choose. Even when we do something we later regret, it makes a difference knowing that we were not just victims of forces in or beyond ourselves.

It is true that some of us have done things we heartily wish we had not had the freedom and the power to do. Yet I confess that I am brought up short when someone tells me that he prefers, in his heart of hearts, not to have the insecurity that goes with freedom and creativity. Here I think we come to a stark choice, a turning-point.

Let us suppose that you were guaranteed a life full of pleasure and no pain, but that this would be at the cost of your creativity. Would you trade creativity for what many regard as bliss or as security? If you say "Yes" I can only respectfully disagree, even while realizing that in the exercise of their freedom to be creative, men have tortured, dispossessed, and destroyed each other with a cruelty that often makes one ashamed of the human race. I would consider any God cruel who could give man creativity and did not. I would say, let human life be short and cruel in the bargain, but let man be man, and not brute. Let man be man and not something that purrs along, its movements in perfect and predictable control. Let man be free to try to reach the limits of his own capacities, to make his own creative world within the orderly realm of nature. But having asserted my own choice, the matter does not end.

I said, "Suppose you were guaranteed . . .", but when I face that possibility, I find it difficult to imagine a world in which everyone had only to turn from one pleasure to another. What does pleasure by itself mean?

Our task is to find not pleasure but experiences which are satisfying. I said "satisfying," not "gratifying," to call attention to the fact that we often find that gratifying experiences may be satisfying as well. Satisfying experiences do not exclude pleasure; they involve more of our living as a whole.

We thus come again to realize that human experiences always form a network. Therefore the fact of life none of us can escape is that to live is to choose some system of experiences, some patterns or values that will tie our lives together and, without throwing away the best we have, open us up to new possibilities.

To live this way means using the Principle of Creativity as a guide. But this leads us to a second basic principle without which life could become a disaster—the Principle of Justice.

Justice, I suggest, not only means being fair to others, but being fair to ourselves. Each of us has a variety of needs and abilities. We do not know how deep-seated our needs are, nor do we know the scope of our abilities. We often do not know exactly when we have found ourselves and many of us never find ourselves. We cannot be fair to ourselves unless we see what we can do by ourselves as we try to satisfy our needs. To do only "what I want when I want it" may seem exciting but to achieve this we must discover how far our abilities will take us. We don't have to be particularly perceptive to realize that we must give up, or postpone, or only partially gratify many of our desires. But we gather such wisdom as we can by linking our desires with our abilities and achieving balance or harmony within our own lives.

Many thinkers would not use the word "justice," for the ideal of harmony within a life. Justice, they say, has to do with relationships among people; or it involves the distribution of goods among persons. I have several reasons for using the term for the individual and his relationship with himself, and for individuals and their relationships with other individuals. To be just to yourself is to treat yourself in such a way that you bring the different dimensions of your life into as much harmony as possible. To be unjust to yourself is to allow yourself to fall short of what it is in you to become. This happens when you feel that some part of you is the slave of another part—"I allowed my anger to get the best of me," for instance.

This is by no means an easy process. But we begin by realizing that we would never be much if we were apart from others. What we become from the first breath we take depends upon how much our parents and others are willing to share with us. Are our parents, our brothers and sisters, the other people around us willing to sacrifice to help us so that we find where we best fit, given our capacities and skills?

We all seem to know what justice means when we are on the receiving end. It means that others must give us the opportunity to become wholesome, as far as it lies within their power to do so. It means that they will not, while we are dependent upon them, use us for their own purposes, and toss us aside when we no longer fit into their own scheme of things.

Immanuel Kant caught the spirit of justice when he said: "Act so that you treat humanity, whether in your own person or in that of another, always as an end and never as a means only." * He was emphasizing the fact that since persons are capable of reason, they are not to

* Immanuel Kant, *Foundations of the Metaphysics of Morals.* (Lewis W. Beck, tr.) New York: Bobbs-Merrill Company, 1969, page 54.

be used as if they cannot reason about what is good for themselves and others.

We must not neglect three corollaries. First, justice is not equal sharing. In human affairs, no two persons, no two human situations are ever equal. John has more ability than Jim and begins life with this headstart, but Jim has learned to work harder and has developed a personality that can stand stress. To be just to either of them is to bear in mind what each needs if he is to grow without needless conflicts. The myth of "the same for everybody" is disastrous in human affairs. Each of us needs different treatment at different points in our growth.

Second, we must realize that since we do have weaknesses and strengths, there is no such thing as a completely self-made man who could be where he is if nobody had ever tried to be just to him.

Third, we work out the need for personal and social justice by agreeing to live by laws which we expect to be enforced as impartially as possible. Our laws reflect our realization that the more frequently different people are involved, the more important it is for each of us to agree to live by a certain standard, even if we do not feel like doing so. Hence, we say, "Let us be equal before the law"; that is, let us assure ourselves that this much we shall insist upon from everyone. In making laws, then, we intend to guarantee a minimum of protection for and responsibility from everyone reached by the law, whether it be the safety standards for our streets and highways, or our freedom to dissent.

What has all this to do with knowing God? In short, why can't we simply believe in a community in which we treat other persons as ends in themselves, and leave it at that? Why be religious?

All great religions have insisted that we must be *at least* good humanists. But they have also insisted that we connect "being human," respecting each other as persons, with the whole of the universe. Thus in the Judeo-Christian faith, God, the Creator-Person cares enough for us to create a realm of nature which nourishes, supports, and challenges us to be creative. As the First Commandment put it, belief in God and belief in our neighbor are part of each other.

It is time to remind ourselves here that the issue each of us faces is the issue Moses confronted. Moses, we recall, had his burning-bush experience as the dramatic outcome of his long agonizing over the problem of his relationship to his fellowmen. A Freudian humanist, however, might explain it this way: Here was a fatherless boy who finally solved the problem of authority in his life by a vision of a cosmic Authority-Figure to whom he could turn as the source of his own moral conviction. There is no more here than his own human yearning to believe that a Sovereign, a Ruler of man and nature, was unwilling to allow the Jews to continue to suffer in servitude to finite power.

The issue between the theist and the humanist is now joined. In the name of man, the humanist resists interpreting experiences (and he admits people have them) that place the authority of freedom and justice upon anything other than man's own being as he comes to grips with the guidelines established by his nature.

I cannot prove that the humanist is wrong. Indeed, I seem to side with him when I agree that the moral law of which we become aware is not a set of principles imposed upon us from outside. Moral law is a guide to what we human beings can and ought to become. But assuming there is a God who is our purposeful, intelligent Creator, how else would he express his aims for us? Certainly not by making men puppets who seem to act by themselves but really are responding to the pulling of strings they know nothing about and are powerless to resist. Because men are free, within limits, to live up to their best, it might seem that this fact expresses it all. A God who made man a robot might be all-powerful but, as I see it, hardly worthy of our worship.

No, I believe that the theist takes the best in the humanist view of man and understands it as God's sharing of his creativity with man. Of course man has his own nature; of course he came into the world at a certain point in evolution and has survived by his fitness to survive among the forces of nature. But what impresses me is not simply that he survived, but that he did so on a microscopic planet. I think, further, that man could not have survived without his willingness to think for himself, to take the risks of creativity, to share with those he could have killed or subjugated, to develop laws as guidelines for social justice and personal fulfillment. Therefore, I join Moses in an "invincible surmise" and say: The universe was made for justice, for freedom and for the fulfillment of creativity, and this is what I see as significant evidence for God.

In other words, man is not an additive to the world. He did not somehow develop in a process of slow evolution those instincts and reflexes that made for survival. Millions of animals at every level have survived only to produce other millions that never could change themselves or their environment in any deliberate, let alone significant, fashion.

Yet among them, but significantly unlike them, there appeared about two million years ago, a creature who was not cast in the image of animals or even of man as we now know him. This creature appeared capable both of *re-lating* himself to other men and to the laws of nature, and also capable of *detaching* himself so that he could take some small early steps that would lead someday to fulfillment for himself and his fellowmen.

With this panorama before us, why not believe in God? It is more intellectual to believe what the humanist believes, that man's nobility and his dream for the future is his only? Why should not the best in man be a clue to the nature of things? Men ought, indeed, to march to their inner drummer, but if they find the beat that allows them to march side-by-side with one another in a world of justice and creativity, why say that the music is theirs alone? It is this reasoning that is supported by other facts about persons-in-nature.

6. Can We Believe in Love Without Believing in God?

There are different approaches to belief in God, but none of them gives us insight into what that belief means in the growth of human beings in this world. I come now to a dimension of human experience which, in connection with our need for knowledge, justice, and creativity, tells us more about ourselves and about God. I am speaking of human love.

No experience encourages us more in creativity and justice than love, and especially that expression of love called forgiveness. To live without being loved and without loving is scarcely living at all. When a person feels loved, and especially by one he admires or upon whom he depends, he finds a confidence and hope that he would not otherwise experience. And if a person never loves, he never experiences the yearning and the challenge to create a special oneness with his beloved.

What, then, do I mean here by "love"? I do not mean to exclude romantic love, in which a strong attachment unites two persons; nor do I wish to exclude friendly love, or parental love, in which there is devotion and mutual trust. But I suspect that romantic, friendly, and parental love are special forms of love. Perhaps the dominant impulse in these forms of love is compassion, which literally means "suffering with." When a person feels compassion

43

for another, it hurts when he cannot help him through a time of suffering.

But the power in love is not emotion by itself, and so I define love at its best as the willingness to accept another's strengths and weaknesses in such a way that evil is minimized and strength grows. Love, then, involves a purpose that dominates one's entire way of life; love is a style of life. The loving person is willing to endanger his own well-being, if necessary, for the sake of the other person. Love is the concern for justice for the other person as a whole. The loving person is not concerned about the other person's paying for his mistakes. Without thinking he can rub out any harm the other may have done, by loving him he can help create a new climate in which the loved one will not feel rejected as a human being.

This is easy to say but difficult to do. Yet everything we know about what helps a person grow after he has hurt someone else, or has been hurt, indicates that he still must feel cared about if he is to recreate an adequate relationship with others. Of course I am talking about you and me. Which of us fails to remember those who gave back to us our faith in ourselves by believing in us in spite of everything—when nothing but darkness seemed to lie ahead?

Jesus, that lover of God and man, gave expression to the dynamics of love in the parable of the prodigal son. The risks, the creativity, of being loved and of loving are revealed if we look beneath the surface of this story.

A young man goes to his father and asks for his inheritance so that he can do his own thing, as we say today. I imagine the father warns him to be careful, but he knows that if his son is to be himself he must go his own way. The son leaves home with his inheritance, but perhaps he is more steeped than he realized in his parents' ways of doing things. His brother stays home to help on the farm, but he may have been envious of his brother's opportunity.

Away from home, the son does as he pleases, sows his wild oats, and checks off his mistakes to experience. But eventually he finds that he has spent his inheritance with the all-too-willing help of "friends." And now he feels alone, forsaken, and shaken.

I wonder: Does he, at this point, realize that whatever the restrictions of his father's house nobody there had simply "used" him? Did he face the likelihood that he, too, had used others? In any case, it is not easy to blame ourselves for our failures. We all are tempted to rationalize, to excuse ourselves, but do our defenses really work? Or are they just ways of numbing the pain and the disappointment?

What I find fascinating is the fact that this prodigal son was able to say, "I will return to my father." Would he have said this if he did not believe his father still loved him and wanted him back? Would he have gone back if he believed that his father would blame him for his mistakes and failures? In other words, there were risks that he had to accept as he turned back. He could not be sure his father would take him back as a member of his household. Perhaps, also, he could almost hear his brother say: "Why should you get a second chance?" In a word, was it naive of the prodigal son to suppose that all he had to do was to pick up and go home, and everything would be all right? What would he do if he were in his father's or his brother's place?

Here, I suggest, is another of those turning-points in life. In this case it concerned the prodigal son's willingness to trust his family to continue to care for him, even as he had been trusted to go forth with freedom—to create or to destroy.

Let me generalize the very human situation we all face when we are prodigal—and the turning point that may be there. When a person fails others, when he hurts others as well, he needs to heal, and time will not only heal, but it will give the person time to think. However, a wound of the spirit, a wound caused by hurting others who needed us cannot be easily healed. We need to feel that others will believe in us enough to treat us not in the light of our weakness only, but also in accordance with our strength and promise. Pity won't do; compassion by itself won't do. What will do is the willingness to allow us to become once again a responsive and responsible member of the family or community.

This quality of loving which is forgiveness also involves the willingness to risk some of the good things of life for the sake of helping someone who has willfully wronged us. Forgiveness is not a sentimental "extra." It is our recognition that, having hurt each other, we still need to help each other grow in spite of our faults. A person who cannot forgive is either a weakling, or less than honest with himself. He turns his back on his own misdemeanors and sins, he forgets his own ingratitude, intolerance, cowardice. In so doing, he shuts the door to a creative experience which our ordinary word, "happiness," does not begin to describe. The word "blessedness" captures the agony and ecstasy we experience when we reach out—as the father of the prodigal son did—in mercy toward another who, recognizing his error, trusts us to help him find himself again, and a worthwhile place among men.

To him who does not know blessedness I have no more to say than this: You have not even begun to enter the promised land. Love is not enough; it must include the blessedness of care-full forgiving. Such love is always one's finest hour, for a person dedicates himself to forging a new spirit of mutuality and sharing that takes into account disappointment, sin, and despair, but also intelligence, courage, humility, and kindness.

I have been saying that creativity and justice can never find their full meaning apart from the love that is forgiveness. I suggest that in human affairs, as in plants, we never can say we know the nature of the seed, or of the bud, or of the flower until we see the full fruit, ripe and ready to produce new seed. Without the spirit of love, life loses its yeastiness, its zest.

We now move toward a conclusion that is almost too good to be true. Why should the sun and the stars make us feel the mystery of the unknown and the awed knowledge that we, in knowing something about them, are involved with them in a larger drama? We may not understand exactly how the telescope brings them closer, but the telescopes are *ours* and they represent our ability to respond to what is out there. Why should we trust our ability to get closer to what is out there—and stop short at saying that our love, too, belongs both to us and to out there?

When we love joyously, seeking new ways of growing with each other, why must we say that love is human and not divine? If loving were something fanciful, something that is only the frosting on our lives, then I could take seriously the view that maybe it all *is* the great illusion. But what Freud and so many others never saw clearly was the inner connection between love and every other potentiality for good in our lives. If people, loving truth, seem to find keys to reality, why, when they love each other, are they not also finding out what reality is? To say that there is a God, and that he loves unto forgiveness, is to affirm just this: It is to hold that nothing is lastingly creative that is not done, as the philosopher Whitehead said, without "the tender care that nothing worth saving is lost."

I have tried to show that we cannot think thoroughly about ourselves without trusting the great surmise that God is the one eternal Being, a Thinker, a Planner, and One who loves.

Next we must take what for many is the only route, and for others a dead end—the direct experience of God. For those who take this route, the paths I have tried to mark out are at best reinforcements of this experience.

When we bear in mind that man, in all the records we have, has never been without a haunting sense of his oneness with a Unity, we know that we must gain some appreciation of what it means to know God directly.

7. Can We Know God Directly?

In the following passage, John Ruskin tries to describe how he experienced the God he found in and through his experiences with nature:

"Lastly, although there was *no definite religious sentiment mingled with it,* there was a continual perception of Sanctity in the whole of nature, *from the slightest thing to the vastest;* an instinctive awe, mixed with delight; an indefinable thrill, such as we sometimes imagine to indicate the presence of a disembodied spirit, I could only *feel this perfectly when I was alone;* and then it would often make me shiver from head to feet with the joy and fear of it, when after being some time away from hills I first get to the shore of a mountain river, where the brown water circled among the pebbles, or when I first saw the swell of distant land against the sunset, or the first low broken wall, covered with mountain moss. *I cannot in the least describe the feeling;* but I do not think this is my fault, nor that of the English language, for I am afraid no feeling is describable. If we had to explain even the sense of bodily hunger to a person who had never felt it, we should be hard put to it for words; and the joy in nature seemed to me to come *of a sort of heart-hunger, satisfied with* the presence of a Great and Holy Spirit . . . These feelings remained in their full intensity till I was eighteen or twenty, and then, as the reflective and practical power increased, and the 'cares of this world' gained upon

me, faded gradually away, in the manner described by Wordsworth in his 'Intimations of Immortality'." * (Italics added.)

In a not too different vein, Wordsworth tried to ar-
ticulate his experience:

> A sense sublime
> Of something far more deeply interfused,
> Whose dwelling is the light of setting suns.
> And the round ocean and the living air
> And the blue sky and in the mind of man ;
> A motion and a spirit which impels
> All thinking things, all objects of all thought.
> And rolls through all things. **

Is this just an esthetic response to the beautiful and the
sublime in nature? Is it the wide-eyed romancing of early
adolescence? Or is it *as well* the "beauty of holiness"? Is it
a response to a Presence that makes a tender spirit re-
sound, as a grand piano resounds to the touch of a master-
pianist?

I cannot answer these questions. I, too, have had experiences like these but I do not know whether I would
have interpreted them as "religious" if I had not already
believed in God. I do not doubt that many young people
have experiences that seem truly "out of this world." They
might not call them religious experiences, but in any case
I suspect that, if they are not crowded out, they gather
around them more mature meanings especially if they are
connected with other experiences.

An experience we all have had will illustrate my point.
We all once met our first girlfriend or boyfriend, and this
girl or boy was "special." Was this because we were

* Quoted from Rudolf Otto, *The Idea of the Holy* (John Harvey, ed.)
Oxford University Press, 1923, page 221. From *Modern Painters*, volume
iii, page 309.
** Quoted by Walter T. Stace, *Mysticism and Philosophy*. New York:
J. B. Lippincott Co., 1960, pages 80, 81.

changing and something about him or her brought out responses which were sexual, tender, compassionate, fearful, angry, wonder-ful? Before we fell in love we didn't dream we could respond thus to another human being. Our entire world seemed new, but it also seemed to have a new place for us; we felt wanted and wanting.

Did this early, fresh, overwhelming, first experience of yours become less meaningful later on in your life? Did it teach you that what you see depends not only on what you can see but on what is there, and what you also believe is there?

I am suggesting that while some experiences are so overwhelming that they become turning points in our lives, these experiences are not less important because we later see them in the wider context of our lives. It may be that we see more than what is there just because we were ready to see and wanted to see what we were convinced we saw.

In all fairness, we also must say that it may well be that until we want to see, we shall overlook some qualities that are there. Many, many people have turning-point, transforming experiences but would not call them religious experiences because they were not ready to believe in God.

Analogies drawn from other experiences will not illumine completely the kind of experience Ruskin describes. Let me underscore what we perhaps can agree upon at this point: What each of us might call our "experience of God" does not come labeled as such, even though we may be gripped by the conviction that it is the Presence of God.

As William James said long ago, there is no way for the mystic to convince one who has not had his experience that his claim is valid. To him who is in love the cool evaluation of someone who is not seems to be sheer blindness, if not perversity. Religion is like a great voyage some believe simply should not be taken. And yet some take it, thinking they will find a new route to the riches of the East and find, instead, a new continent. Perhaps this is one reason St. Paul wrote to the Hebrews that, "Now faith is assurance of things hoped for, a conviction of things not seen." (*The New English Bible* translates this as, "And what is Faith? Faith gives substance to our hopes, and makes us certain of realities we do not see.")

At this point in our reasoning, it is not surprising for us to say that the world around us will remain a mystery no matter how much we try to fathom it and yet, to be human is to keep probing in hope and sometimes in despair. Job, a mythical, biblical figure, did not belittle the evil that could befall a man. In the midst of his inability to see any justice in his life, Job heard God out of the tempest of his soul as he contemplated the awesome world about him. Do you fall into the same mood, especially after you have been trying to figure things out, but in vain?

Chapters 38–42 of the Book of Job tell us something important about our quest for meaning:

> "Then the Lord answered Job out of the tempest:
> Who is this whose ignorant words
> Cloud my design in darkness?
> Brace yourself and stand up like a man;
> I will ask questions, and you shall answer.
> Where were you when I laid the earth's foundations?
> Tell me, if you know and understand.
>
> "Who settled its dimensions? Surely you should know.
> Who stretched his measuring-line over it?
> On what do its supporting pillars rest?
> Who set its corner-stone in place,
> When the morning stars sang together
> And all the sons of God shouted aloud? . . .

"Have you comprehended the vast expanse of the world? . . .

"Can you find the cluster of the Pleiades or loose
Orion's belt? . . .
Did you proclaim the rules that govern the heavens,
Or determine the laws of nature on earth? . . .

"Then the Lord said to Job:
Is it for a man who disputes with the Almighty to be
stubborn?
Should he that argues with God answer back?
And Job answered the Lord:
What reply can I give thee, I who carry no weight?
I put my finger to my lips . . .
Then the Lord answered Job out of the tempest:
"Brace yourself and stand up like a man;
I will ask the questions and you shall answer.
Dare you deny that I am just
or put me in the wrong that you may be right? . . ."
(There follows a long catalogue of the power of God to do
what no other Being can do.)

"Then Job answered the Lord:
I know that thou canst do all things
And that no purpose is beyond thee.
But I have spoken of great things which I have
not understood,
Things too wonderful for me to know.
I knew of thee then only by report but now
I see thee with my own eyes" (*New English Bible*).

For many this passage puts into words the ongoing con-
tinuing struggle of the man of faith. Convinced that he is
a child of God, that God does want him to stand upon his
feet like a man, he is nevertheless overwhelmed by the
enormity of a world that defies his imagination.

We often feel this way if at night we stand alone in
complete darkness on a country hill, and feel so small
amidst the stars that pepper the sky embracing our planet.

Which of us does not know the dark night of our thinking, hard-working minds when, in a mood somewhere between humor and despair, we say, "What a fool I am to think that my mind can fathom it all." With the mathematician-philosopher, Blaise Pascal, we may say, "I am a reed, but a thinking reed." How preposterous to suppose that our thoughts can grasp reality! And then Pascal's expression of his own experience comes back: "Thou would'st not seek me, hads't thou not already found me."

Too often we think of the religious experience as one outside of intellect. I suggest there is a conviction of the intellect that the lost can be found.

The passages I have quoted offer examples of experiences in which what is ordinary does not lose its ordinary meaning, but is seen as a sign of a Reality. As an Indian mystic expressed it: "As you practice meditation you may see in vision forms resembling snow, crystal, wind, smoke, fire, lightning, fireflies, the sun, the moon. These are signs that you are on the way to revelation of Brahman" (the One).

Yet many mystics speak of an experience compared to which these experiences seem to be just the way up the mountain, not the peak itself. When we can persevere and get to the top, even our own body and all of our will seem "lost." As we read such passages, we must remember that these writers are suggesting that what they describe is beyond ordinary meaning. There is a joy, a blessedness, a rapture—words that mean "I feel wonder-ful," or "I am no longer, for there is nothing I experience that I can connect with any of my usual experiences. So St. Theresa wrote:

During the rapture itself the body is very often as if it were dead, perfectly powerless. It continues in the position it was in when the rapture came upon it—if sitting, sitting . . . For though the senses fail but rarely, it has happened to me occasionally to lose them wholly . . . for a short time. . . . But in general there remains the power of hearing and seeing; but it is as if the things heard and seen were at a great distance, far away . . . *I do not say that the soul sees and hears when the rapture is at its highest—when the faculties are lost because profoundly united with God—for then it neither sees nor hears nor perceives . . . This utter transformation of the soul continues only for an instant.* (Italics added.) *

The important point is not whether the usual sensory experience is subdued, for the final state is clearly beyond the sensory, and it transforms the person's view of himself and what is real to him.

A ninth-century Islamic mystic, Abu Yazid al-Bistami, spoke of the "Great Silence." The contrast extends to the realm of values as well as sense beyond good and evil:

"Be in a domain where neither good nor evil exists; both of them belong to the world of created things; in the presence of Unity there is neither command nor prohibition.

"All this talk and turmoil and noise and movement is outside of the veil; within the veil is silence and calm and rest." **

And Ibu Sina (d. A.D. 1037) described earlier stages of

---

* Quoted by W. T. Stace in *Mysticism and Philosophy*, page 51, from *Life of St. Theresa*, D. Lewis, 1924, Chapter 20.
** As quoted by W. T. Stace, *The Teachings of the Mystics*. New York: The New American Library (Mentor Books), page 205.

mystical life and the attachment to the good of sense, intellect, and morality as preparation for the final stages of seeing "God in all things . . . then in the fifth stage he becomes accustomed to God's Presence, the brief flashes of lightning become a shining flame, and he attains to direct knowledge of God and is continually in fellowship with him. . . .

"Then he turns to the world of Reality and his contemplation of God is stable and continuous, and *when he passes from striving to attainment,* his inmost soul becomes a polished mirror reflecting the fact of God." * (Italics added.)

It should be clear that the mystic is not disdainful of the world, and of higher stages of morality. Rather, he wants us to realize that neither "the truth" nor "the good" is to be restricted to these stages. Indeed, his life is not *in* them or to be identified *with* them, for truth and goodness come to fulfillment in his peak-experience of God, the promontory from which he can see everything else in perspective.

Another way of putting the claim that once God has been experienced everything else is transformed, is to say that God is the Void, the Nothing, the Abyss—meaning that this Reality is empty of the things, values, and character which make up what we call "reality" because we do not know better.

Thus Lao-Tzu (*circa* 570 b.c.), founder of Taoism, wrote:

"There are ways but the Way is uncharted;
There are names but not nature in words:
Nameless indeed is the source of creation

* Quoted from W. T. Stace, *The Teachings of the Mystics*, pages 206–207.

But things have a mother and she has a name."
Again:
The way is a Void,
Used but never filled
An abyss it is,
Like an ancestor
From which all things come. *

Plotinus, who was born about 205 A.D. in Egypt but settled in Rome, was a philosopher much affected by his mystical experience and his study of mysticism. In his view God did not *create* the world and man; God is the One from whom everything that is *emanates*. The farther away the emanating rays are from the center of the One, the less "reality" is in them. Thus once more our task, said Plotinus, is not to lose ourselves in the lower levels of ordinary things and values, but to know what it means to be at one with the One:

"Here the greatest, the ultimate test is set before our souls; all our toil and trouble is for this, not to be left without a share in the best of visions. The man who attains this is blessed in seeing that blessed sight, and he who fails to attain it has failed utterly. A Man has not failed if he fails to win beauty of colours or bodies, or power or office or kingship even, but if he fails to win this and only this. . . . When he sees the beauty in bodies, he must not run after them; we must know that they are images, traces, shadows, and hurry away to That which they image. . . . Let all these things go, and do not look. Shut your eyes and change to and wake another way of seeing *which everyone has but few use.*
"When the Soul is so blessed, and is come to it, or rather when it manifests its presence, when the Soul turns away from visible things and makes itself as beautiful as possible

* Quoted by W. T. Stace, *The Teachings of the Mystics*, New York: The New American Library (Mentor Book), page 104.

and becomes like the One (the manner of preparation and adornment is known to those who practice it) and seeing the One suddenly appearing in itself, for there is nothing between, *nor are they any longer two, but one. . . .*" * (Italics added.)

In many passages, mystics express themselves in terms of unity, of identity, of part with whole. This view is called "monistic" since the oneness of all and the identity of everything with the One is paramount. We will later ask whether this experience of God is to be accepted, or whether a different interpretation does not make more sense. Mystics themselves do not agree with each other as to how identity is to be understood. They even express themselves as if they are of two minds on this point.

A special example is the great mystic, St. John of the Cross (1542–1591). Like others he stresses the emptying "of all these imagined forms, figures, and images," for the soul "must remain in darkness in respect to these internal senses if it is to attain Divine union." *

The word "darkness" is used in the sense of empty, void, abyss. But the phrase, "dark night of the soul," has another meaning that Christian mystics, in particular, emphasize. This "dark night" suggests also that man is not identified with God as part-of-whole but that *the union of the soul with God is a union of love and likeness, not division of substance.* ** The mystic undergoes despair because he does not "get through" and thinks that he has been rejected:

* From Plotinus, *Enneads.* As quoted by W. T. Stace, *The Teaching of the Mystics,* pages 113, 114.
** As quoted by W. T. Stace, *The Teachings of the Mystics,* page 185.

"But what the sorrowing soul feels most painfully in this condition is the dreadful thought that God has abandoned it and has flung it into utter darkness . . . it feels most vividly the shadows and laments of death and the torments of hell which consist in the conviction that God in his anger has chastized and forsaken it forever." *

It is quite likely that union here is interpreted to be the goal of a fellowship, and not as an identity in which the first person is lost. In such a union the participants both have the same goal, and they carry it out together. In the instance of "the dark night," God is the Being who withholds the grace of his presence, not because he is trying to punish the individual, but because the individual has been unfaithful to the conditions of union. Plotinus, for example, suggests that God shines upon our souls as the sun does upon windows, but our windows are not clear. Plotinus' actual words shift from one meaning to another as he says, "the Divine light of the Being of God is unceasingly *beating upon it, or, to use a better expression, the Divine light* is ever dwelling in it" (the soul).

The context is clear: the individual must conform to the main conditions—purity and love—in return for having the light come fully into his life and illuminate it. "This abyss of wisdom greatly exalts and enriches the soul and places it at the very source of the science of love." **

Such passages remind us that as we read the mystics we must remember that their religious lives had ups and downs, movement and progress, and that they were solving problems on this level even as they tried to live their entire

* *Ibid.*, page 187.
** Quoted by W. T. Stace in *Teachings.* . . . , pages 188 and 197.

lives in the light of their progress. They suffered as most of us suffer. Thus Plotinus said:

> "There is yet another reason why the soul has walked securely in this darkness, and this is because its way has been a way of suffering. For the road of suffering is far more secure and profitable than that of rejoicing and of action; first, because in suffering man receives added strength from God, while in action and in any kind of fruition the soul is indulging its own weaknesses and imperfections; and second, because in suffering the soul activates the virtues and thus becomes purer, wiser, and more cautious." *

We must not neglect this view of suffering which, as Plotinus said, we endure in "the dark night of the soul." The soul is now, as it were, undergoing a cure, so that it may regain its health. **

The final passages we quote come from two modern mystics. The first, Arthur Koestler, does not interpret his experiences in terms of the great theological perspectives we have been sampling, but he, too, speaks of losing his individuality in the "universal pool." That Koestler, who had been a fervent Communist from 1931 to 1938, was transformed by his mystical experience is made clear in the *The Invisible Writing*, the second volume of his autobiography, *Arrow in the Blue*:

> "When I say 'the I had ceased to exist,' I refer to a concrete experience that is verbally as incommunicable as the feeling aroused by a piano concerto, yet just as real—only much more real. In fact, its primary mark is the sensation that this state is more real than any other one has experienced before —that for the first time the veil has fallen and one is in

* From Stace, *Teachings. . . . ,* page 195.
** *Ibid.,* page 195.

touch with 'real reality,' the hidden order of things, the X-ray texture of the world, normally obscured by layers of irrelevancy. . . .
It was as if a massive dose of vitamins had been injected into the veins. Or, to change the metaphor, I resumed my travels . . . like an old car with its batteries freshly recharged." *

The experience gave Koestler a "direct certainty that a higher order of reality existed, and that it alone invested existence with meaning." Koestler tries to express the total impact of his experience in the following metaphor:

"The captain of a ship sets out with a sealed order in his pocket which he is only permitted to open on the high seas. He looks forward to the moment which will end all uncertainty; but when the moment arrives and he tears the envelope open, he only finds an invisible text which defies all attempts at chemical treatment. Now and then a word becomes visible, or a figure denoting a meridian; then it fades again. He will never know the exact wording of the order; nor whether he has complied with it or failed in his mission. But his awareness of the order in his pocket, even though it cannot be deciphered, makes him think and act differently from the captain of a pleasure cruiser or of a pirate ship. I also like to think that the founders of religions, prophets, saints and seers had at moments been able to read a fragment of the invisible text; after which they had so much padded, dramatised, and ornamented it, that they themselves could no longer tell what parts of it were authentic." **

Albert Schweitzer, whose life-style we associate with the words "reverence for life," wrote in his book, *Civilization*

---

* Quoted by Stace, *Teachings* . . . , page 233.
* Quoted by Stace in *Teaching* . . . , page 235.

and Ethics: "I live my life in God, in the mysterious ethical divine personality which I cannot discover in the world, but only experience in myself as a mysterious impulse." *
Later in the same book he wrote:

> "Just as a wave has no existence of its own, but is part of the continual movement of the ocean, thus I also am destined never to experience my life as self-contained but always as part of the experience which is going on around me."

This is the same Albert Schweitzer who gave his life to the under-privileged in Africa as a medical missionary. It is he who remarked: "There are no heroes of action; only heroes of renunciation and suffering." ** He knew what was meant by the words: "Anyone who proposes to do good must not expect people to roll stones out of his way, but must accept his lot calmly, if they even roll a few more upon it." ***

There can be no doubt that the religious and the mystical experience bring to those who undergo them such a new sense of the meaning of their lives that they feel transformed. They have vision and strength they never thought possible. They are not alone; they are identified with God. Does this mean that in the mystical experience they literally lose themselves in God? Some of them certainly have said so. But it seems clear that they "go up and down," and that the "dark night" emphasizes that they do not lose their individuality and freedom. They must read the order in the invisible text as well as possible.

This interpretation of mystical experience defines

* Albert Schweitzer, *Civilization and Ethics*, New York, Macmillan Co., 1929 p. xvi.
** Albert Schweitzer, *Out of My Life and Thought*. New York: New American Library, 1933, page 75.
*** *Ibid.*, page 112.

identity as finding oneself in relation to the aims of God for each of us. It emphasizes our personal responsibility, as we interact with God, for the good and evil that develops because we are creators. It places the responsibility for good and evil on both men and God.

8. If God Is Good, Why Is There Evil?

There are two kinds of evil. The first is moral evil, and the second is natural evil. Human beings cannot be held responsible for natural evils, for cyclones, earthquakes, and other phenomena that destroy living things or make life all but intolerable. We have emphasized the importance to human welfare of the orderly sequences without which man can neither survive nor build, nor plan his future. It will rain; it will stop raining; the sun will shine; night will give way to day and day to night. We take for granted the billions of ways in which we depend upon the order that we did not make. It is the disorder that creates chaos, and illness, and it is death that takes us by surprise.

I cannot accept the view that if we knew enough, we would see that evil, in a larger sense, is part of the greater good. However, there is much truth in this. We know that hardships help us appreciate our blessings and contribute to our strength as persons. Even so, I must point out that the same can be said of goodness: "If we knew enough, we would know that this good is part of a larger evil." For example, children brought up with good care by good parents are not necessarily better off when they have to face difficulties themselves. A person blinded in adolescence does not find it easier to accept than the person born blind. No, natural evils cannot be put aside in the hope that they are part of a larger good.

Indeed, as we noted in the last chapter, some of the mystics urged us to get beyond the good and evil of this world because this world was only partially real. They seemed to think that this solves the problem. But does it? When these mystics return to this world, they still have to live with the world's good and its evil.

No mystical experience, I suggest, can support the view that justice is injustice, that love is hate, that illness is better than health. It is one thing to say that in and through our experience of God we can find more power and a more profound perspective that will keep us from despair when things go wrong, and from false pride when things go well. But no experience of God can dull our sensitivity to the tragedies that overcome both the evil and the good, despite anything we can do. Natural events are the source of good in our lives, but they are also the source of evil that we cannot by any stretch of the imagination say men deserve. Can the Person-Creator be good and willingly allow such natural evils? We cannot dodge this question, but let us first examine what is involved in moral evil, that is, the evil men do because they abuse their freedom and intelligence.

Here we face the meaning of life itself. Earlier we asked this question: If we had the choice of being conscious, well-oiled machines or robots, and if, furthermore, we were guaranteed no pain and a variety of pleasures, would we choose this at the cost of our freedom and creativity?

The answer to this question makes all the difference in the world if we also ask: If God is omnipotent and good, that is, if he is capable of doing everything worthwhile, why did he give us the freedom we have if he knew that we could then kill each other, torture each other in body and in mind, enslave each other? Why did he condemn human beings to freedom when they knew so little that they were also condemned to uncertainty and anxiety?

Some philosophers and scientists reject the notion of freedom to choose in the sense we are using it here. They do so, in part, because they think that unless we can predict what we shall do, we must despair of understanding man and of controlling the stresses and strains which threaten the growth of personality. And some theologians deny that man has any freedom in order to assure us that nothing we can do will keep God's goals from being accomplished. For these theologians, the denial of human freedom protects the complete power, goodness, and foreknowledge of God. For many philosophers and scientists the denial of human freedom protects the possibility of humanly predicting, and controlling, the future. Nevertheless, as long as man's knowledge is so limited that he does not know the future, anxiety exists. And I fear that an attempt to decrease anxiety by erasing freedom would encourage people to manipulate others as though they were only complicated things. Either way, the kind of goodness that makes life worthwhile, the goodness born of creative freedom to choose, is undermined.

It seems clear, then, that we cannot escape from uncertainty and anxiety. But to affirm the freedom of choice we have *as persons* is to grant man the power to help shape his own future, without denying that in realizing this freedom he must use law and order not of his own making. We must grant, as we have in our discussion of natural evil, that there are conditions by which the individual, even after he has grown to the age of understanding, is all but trapped. But most of us, had we been willing to make sacrifices, could have made the most of a lesser good, could have given up a preferred good that was not within reach without despair or self-pity. Most of us can look back and in all honesty say: "Yes, if I had been willing to take that harder road, I would be better off now."

Day by day we know that while we are not free to change many things, we are able to change our own inner attitudes. We can brighten the corner where we are, if we cannot change that corner. We cannot change what happens to us, but we can change our attitude toward what happens.

One day I referred to one of my students, who was seriously paralyzed by polio, as crippled. He looked at me and said: "I am handicapped, but I'm not crippled." How right he was!

If you can agree with the conclusion that the most precious good we have is that of being co-creators, the problem of evil then becomes the problem of good-and-evil. Better to be the kind of beings who have a hand in making our own futures, in reshaping the world and each other, than to have no hand in our future at all.

In making her choices about your development, your mother may have made mistakes, but you can be glad that she could help to shape you. Now it is open to all of us, always within limits, to re-shape ourselves. When we appreciate our role as co-creators, we recognize that much of the evil in our world is caused by a good—the fact that we can create. We also realize that much of the good is caused by our individual creativity and by our freedom to cooperate with others. We are co-creators with God, with our parents, with our society. We also are free to use the good we could not have had without them for our own destructive purposes—and in the name of self-development.

There is one experience we all find extremely hard to bear. We have worked hard at building something or at taking care of something, in the hope that it would be of value both to ourselves and to someone else. Then someone comes along and, without realizing it, destroys it. Most of the time we accept these disasters, for we realize that they were accidents. But when someone knowingly destroys what we have built so that he can do as he wishes, or can "express himself," we find this almost impossible to bear.

Still—would we really have it otherwise? I suggest that moral evil, the abuse we willfully inflict on each other, is a part of any system in which persons are allowed to grow. Would any of us, in a calm and reflective mood, give up the insecurity that growing up involves, plus the creative insecurity of freedom?

To grow is to be insecure; neither infant nor adolescent nor adult knows what the next stage is to bring. And because we don't grow like blades of grass, or lilies of the field, or tomatoes—or even dogs and seals—we know the meaning of enduring fear and anxiety, and we have to live with our mistakes. To be free within limits is to be insecure because we do not know enough and because we are free to do evil. But through it all we know also the gratifications and satisfactions that come with working things out, enjoying our dreams, fostering our hopes, and living in faith. We could not do this if all order depended on us. In growing we need nature's guidelines, the guidelines of the family and society we live in, the guidelines we find in our own unique selves—all guidelines that keep us on the tracks as we decide where we shall extend or change those tracks.

We come from a different direction, then, to the considerations we mentioned when we were talking about the prodigal son. We are in a world where the basic conditions make it possible for us to be born, move about, select what we wish from life. At the same time, we are sifted out by an order of nature which is the same for all of us. God has provided the same basic laws for life, for health, for the just and the unjust. Some theologians refer to this as "general providence;" we don't create it, but we can't live and learn without it. The more knowing we become, the more wisely we can choose what we shall do about ourselves and about this world that no human being created, but that belongs to God. He does not make our choices for us because he wants us to be co-creators in shaping and reshaping our lives, our societies, even the physical world about us. He knows that in our attempts to be creative, we can poison the air others must breathe, physically and morally. We can pollute our physical environment, needlessly destroy living things, and act as if we were the last creatures on this earth. Thus we can ask for our inheritance and then proceed to destroy it.

This is the gloomy side of the picture, and this is not all. Those who would be free have a special contempt for themselves when they know that they have enslaved themselves and are chained by their own habits and attitudes. We must not minimize how deep this despair can be. Many of us have a very difficult time developing an attitude that helps us to see our very real faults, place them in perspective, look upon them with a sense of humor. We feel not only left out by others but also unworthy even of those who love us. We need to learn much more about helping people at every stage of their lives, about accepting their limitations, about being deeply sorry for the evil they have done to themselves and to others. This is easier to say than to do. But above all, I have suggested, a person needs someone to believe in him, to encourage him without overdoing it, to help him rebuild his life on what is still good. We need to quarantine evil everywhere, when we cannot overcome it.

This is the time for me to repeat that part of the evidence for God is the fact that we *can* heal, and heal best and lastingly through being loved and loving. I am not discounting for a moment the importance of the power to change that comes when we can allow God, the Creator and Sustainer, to strengthen us.

Much of what I have been saying about evil has forced us to realize once more that we cannot define either goods or evils, apart from some guiding idea of what makes our lives most satisfying to us. To live without having freedom to become what we think is best costs less than to live like pleasure machines, or beings who would never suffer because they are so made that they cannot participate in their own growth. Yet, as we have seen, freedom is a heady wine. Drunk with ourselves, we fail to realize that loving and being loved is never just like eating and drinking. Being loved fails if we ourselves never appreciate it enough to *love* (not *like*) *ourselves* and, therefore, live the more complete life in which we care for and can accept care from others.

The world of love, I repeat, is one we alone can create; neither God nor man can make us love, and if they could we would not be loving. Loving calls for imagination, patience, and the willingness to be disappointed by our own failures and the lack of appreciation by those we love—all as we try to build the foundations of a creative community of responsible persons.

I am suggesting that because there is no other way of preserving or creating the best we know about living in this world, we have in the principle of loving and being loved the firmest grip on what the world is all about. We can see a theme being worked out in the history of the world. As Rollo May, the psychiatrist, has said, the opposite of love is not hate; it is indifference. The world we live in is a world in which indifference would mean that every person would think only of himself, and that would mean chaos and misery. Hate, too, means chaos and misery, because people love without vision, or they care more about being loved than about creating a community of love.

On these grounds I affirm once again that in spite of man's inhumanity to man, which is the cause of human evil, the world is basically good. It is a world in which the source of creativity is in being loved and loving. This is what I think the Christian means when he says that God is love, or the Buddhist means when he says that if he is on the way to heaven and sees one person suffering on earth, he will return to help the suffering. Heaven is helping one another grow. In this way we find ourselves "at one" with God.

So much for the moral evil which is a product of both God's and man's concern that free creativity be encouraged. We can think of God's love as being perfect because he would have us share in the creativity he supremely knows. But when we think of the natural evil for which man cannot be blamed, I think we shall need to refine our traditional view of God.

When the traditional theist holds before us the vision of God as the Creator and Sustainer of the world and man, we think of a Sovereign King of all there is. In this vision of excellence, God's omnipotence is not the preposterous kind that is supposed to square a circle or make a mountain without a valley. God is all-wise, merciful, and just.

But there is more to this vision of perfection, and it comes out when we ask whether natural evil affects God as well as man. Does God's perfection keep him from being affected by the fact that finite creatures suffer in ways that cannot, by any reasonable stretch of the imagination, be said to do them good? The traditional view is that a perfect Being does not depend in any way upon what his creatures can do, or suffer. His will be done. It brooks no interference. To say that he suffers, too, that he is influenced by evil, is to suppose that he is not in control of all there is, or that he must overcome some defect in himself. There are impressive theoretical reasons for holding to a belief in a God who indeed transcends the world and everything in it that lives, hopes, loves, enjoys, and suffers.

That this is not the only way in which God's perfection may be conceived is clear from the Judeo-Christian tradition. For God now comes into our midst as the promised Messiah, for the Jews, and as the Redeemer and Savior, for the Christian. Speaking from the Christian point of view, for the moment, we ask: Does the Christian mean what he says when he talks of God taking the shape of imperfect man, suffering from the evil that men do, even to death on a cross? Does Jesus, the Son of man and the Son of God—that phase of God that comes in the flesh to show us what we can be—show us in his suffering on the cross that God suffers when we sin? Does not all this, then, suggest that something is happening to the idea of perfection?

Why not take another look at our doctrine of perfection, and realize that perhaps in this very emphasis on love and creativity another vision of excellence is emerging. Perfection now means not completion but progressive creativity; it means not overriding and absolute power, but the power that is found in loving and giving. It means creating over and over again in order to increase the good already achieved. What looms before our imagination now is a Person indeed powerful enough to be the Creator and Sustainer of heaven, earth, and all living beings, but who is not satisfied by the lordly manner, by having full sway. His essence consists of creating free creatures and using his power in every way possible to work in and for a world where people can be co-creators in love. He is indeed closer to us in some ways than our hands and feet, but not as the all-powerful king. He does not force himself upon us; it is up to us to become one with him and to grasp his vision of mutual, long-suffering love and forgiveness.

In this view, God is not perfect in the traditional absolute sense. How could this be if his will for us and our society can be held back by our short-sightedness, by the very fact that we must grow in love, and love in growth? This God prefers to work, as far as possible, and in ways beyond our comprehension, with every created being who can grow in any way.

Does this mean that God can fail? Yes, in each of our lives insofar as we refuse to be creative, but not, so far as we know, as the Creator and Sustainer of the order we find in the world. He may seem to fail here and there—cyclones, cancers of mind and body seem to indicate this. But he never fails to work for the best possible community of creators.

I am frequently asked how we can know this. My reply is that we can be no more certain of this than the evidence allows. But the very evidence I have drawn together for God's existence is also evidence of his increasing creativity. After all, life did appear on earth; the entire process of evolution testifies to greater flexibility in living beings, ending in man's capacity to be more creative and more destructive than any other being. This is a "vale of soul-making," and if the process of evolution sometimes seems to falter, taken as a whole, the trend is upward.

But we still must ask: Does the evil rooted in the imperfections no human being can help, does such excess, such undisciplined evil, become more understandable? Why would a Creator-God, wise enough to know what evils some of his creations can inflict and what misfortunes they must endure, allow himself to create a world in which these things take place?

Would not a good God forego creativity if it could mean excruciating hell? Surely, if God is good, and if such evils exist—and they do—surely God is not perfect in power.

From the point of view of absolute perfection, a creative God of love who nevertheless creates beings who can produce hell on earth may seem to be a limited God, especially if he cannot seem to keep evil from appearing. Furthermore, we assume that the only kind of perfection is the "absolute" kind, and if we have lived with that view, it might seem better not to believe in God at all than to believe in a God who can allow such a mess—even in the name of creative variety.

I myself believe that we cannot adequately explain the excess of evil in the world without presenting an aspect of God's nature with which he is struggling—and has struggled victoriously, as the total evolutionary process and development of man shows.

In the last analysis, I rest my case on both the moral and religious impetus in our lives. I admit that neither view of perfection explains the problem of excess evil; nevertheless, I find an absolute God more worthy of admiration than of worship. For I am told that this God in his wisdom, power, and goodness is beyond all insecurity. If I accept the absolutist view, this means that God does create being after being, but never knows what it is to fail, to waver, or to grow. His "love" could then scarcely be creative, once each being is created, for there would be no disappointment to overcome. Hence, there is no real sharing by God in the growth of his creatures.

Indeed, some theologians tell us that God's love is not a wanting love, but an over-flowing love that is influenced by nothing it produces, and that needs no love in return. In this view, creation is the process of bringing many imperfect creators into being but never being affected by them. At the same time, I am told that God knows what it means for human beings to grow, to suffer from despair, from disappointment, and from sin.

Let me assume, then, that there are some evils that so far are beyond the scope of human or divine power. Religion now becomes our working with God, in every effort, to keep evil from spreading, to be creative even though this may mean disappointment and despair. Yet is not this God of creative love worthy of worship and of loyalty? This question I must leave with my reader.

As we come to the close of this chapter and this book I hope that we have become more aware that "the experience of God" is not a simple matter. Perhaps we can understand why able and honest minds do not experience or believe in God, and why believers themselves disagree with each other and differ in their conception of what perfection means.

My own seeking, through this book, leaves me all the more convinced that:

1) The very search for truth presupposes that our finite minds are not aliens in a world indifferent to our capacities.

2) There is no good more important to persons than the freedom to be either creative or destructive.

3) People will be more destructive than creative unless they accept love and become loving.

You may ask, "Is this what you mean by the experience of God?" It is *at least* this, I reply. The direct experience, the "living awareness" of God, can hardly be taken seriously if our efforts for truth, for justice, for love, for creativity, are dashed. That direct experience confirms what so many of our other creative ventures already point toward. In our everyday lives, that experience means that in the very midst of good and evil we are not alone. God works for himself and with us. We work for ourselves and with each other and with him.

This is not a world for those who will not take the risks involved in creating a community of people who respect each other, care for each other's growth, appreciate nature, and seek to find God in everything. Such persons are not merely happy, they are beyond happiness; they are blessed. And their own blessedness is the best evidence I know that this is a world in which only creators can thrive—because a Creator is at work in it, even in the midst of suffering. Faith is the loving and creative response to that larger Creativity. In this experience we discover peace, but "not as the world giveth."